www.leannegelish.com
substack.saltwithsoul.com
Cover Photography by Leanne Gelish

Letter from Leanne

Sitting at the beach's edge where the sea meets the sand, I crinkle my toes as the cool water meets them. The salt air allows me to breathe deep, and the soft thump of my retriever's tail keeps my breathing in rhythm.

Peace.

It is the most sought-after feeling I've experienced during this last cycle of seasons. Through a painful divorce and an even more painful rediscovery of self, I found calm at the beach. It was my refuge and where I wrote most of this book.

During a time of so much uncertainty, the vastness of the water reminded me that there was room to grow, change, and begin again. After all, no two waves meet the sand the same way. It was then that I decided to start again.

Healing is not a linear journey with a direct endpoint. It takes monumental courage to want to improve yourself: to heal old wounds while doing the work to prevent catastrophic new ones. To heal is to grow; growth is like the horizon when the water meets the sky. It is infinite, and there's always a further point we can meet.

I'm re-publishing this book in 2024, even more different than I was when this was written. The poems enclosed were the only way I could metabolize everything I was experiencing. It was all that came to when I sat to write.

This book is an unconventional love story because it's one where we fall in love with ourselves. We all need to love ourselves, and I hope these words help you find the courage to do so.

The Journal

Journaling is one of the most profound acts of self love. It allows us to be vulnerable, honest, and unapologetically ourselves. As we navigate our lives' intricate tapestry, journaling is a loyal companion.

Pouring our innermost thoughts onto the pages provides a cathartic release, allowing us to untangle the complexities of our minds. It becomes a safe space where we can confront our fears, celebrate our successes, and navigate life's challenges. Through this process, we gain clarity and a deeper understanding of ourselves.

Journaling serves as a compass for personal growth. By revisiting past entries, we witness the evolution of our thoughts and emotions over time. This retrospective insight enables us to identify patterns, recognize triggers, and make informed life decisions. It becomes a roadmap for self improvement, fostering mindfulness and intentionality.

In a world often characterized by hustle and bustle, the quiet ritual of putting pen to paper offers a grounding and meditative practice discovery.

Each poem is followed by a journal page, an affirmation, and a gratitude page. It's outlined to help you change your mindset and care for yourself. At the end are Gratitude and Journal Prompts in case you feel stuck.

The only way to find our calling is to spend time with ourselves, and I hope this book helps you start that journey.

Leanne

Dedicated to all the souls who feel misunderstood:

We are the secret keepers of the ultimate happiness.

Dedicated to the man who inspired Summer: *thank you for giving me the feeling of love all year round.*

Summer

on love

Reflection

I am deserving of all good things life has to offer.

Reflection

Gratitude List

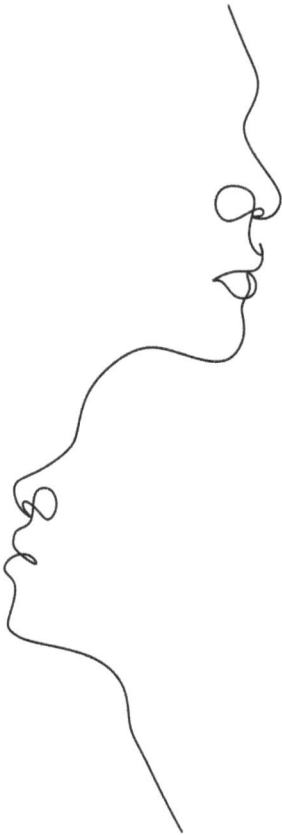

When my soul feels lost,

Roaming the unknown,

My soul knows you,
and it returns home.

Reflection

I am deserving of all good things life has to offer.

Reflection

Gratitude List

Behind the bar, our tale begins,
A friendly banter,
where laughter spins.
You, the regular with stories untold,
Me, the bartender, mixing secrets and gold.
In every order, a chance to connect,
A subtle spark, emotions reflect.
Ice clinks, glasses raise, conversations unfold,
Love brewing silently,
a story to be told.

Reflection

I am worthy of success and prosperity.

Reflection

Gratitude List

Today, thoughts of you,
A familiar feeling, nothing new.
By the shore, uncertain and true,
Feelings awry, a sentimental view.
Remembering the day we played,
In bay waves, memories laid.
We laughed, we danced, a charming chance,
Entranced by a fleeting glance.

You were not mine that day, but I always knew:

One day my heart would be consumed by you.

Reflection

I trust that the universe has a plan for me.

Reflection

Gratitude List

Tracing circles, so light,
Love songs whispered, in the night.
Dreams exchanged, vulnerabilities
laid bare,
In the futility of our spark we dared.
No worry if this our story arc,
Together, we navigate love's embark.

Reflection

I am resilient, and I can overcome any obstacle.

Reflection

Gratitude List

I do not suffer from a foolish heart,
I simply see that love is art.

Reflection

I am resilient, and I can overcome any obstacle.

Reflection

Gratitude List

You are the soft sand that comforts me.
The melodic tune that beats in my heart.
You are the warmth that envelops me.

You are my home.

Reflection

Today, I will approach challenges with a positive mindset.

Reflection

Gratitude List

Many moons pass by,
No swoon in heart's sky.
Decluttered space found,
Butterflies now abound.

Reflection

I am grateful for the abundance in my life.

Reflection

Gratitude List

Love within abides,
With you,
the tide swells,
the lighthouse guides.

Reflection

I release all self-doubt and embrace my worthiness.

Reflection

Gratitude List

The words you say are poetry,
an iambic pentameter set to my heartbeat.
You are a muse on fire,
my love for you only ascends,
my wish is for us to be more than friends.

Reflection

I am open to receiving abundance in all areas of my life.

Reflection

Gratitude List

In friendship's embrace, a journey begins,
A subtle shift where a new chapter spins.
Through laughter and shared dreams,
we find a connection deeper, the heart aligned.
Simple gestures, a touch that lingers,
Unspoken words, heartbeats as singers.
In familiar faces, a newfound grace,
A best friend's love, a warm embrace.
From shared secrets to glances so sweet,
Love blooms quietly, beneath friendship's feat.
In simple moments, the truth unfolds,
Falling in love with the best friend we hold.

Reflection

I am open to receiving abundance in all areas of my life.

Reflection

Gratitude List

I believe when you as the universe for
something,
it will come true.
Everyday, I ask her for you.

Reflection

Today, I will face my fears with courage.

Reflection

Gratitude List

Moments of doubt cross my mind,
as I remember that love is blind.

Reflection

I am surrounded by opportunities for growth and learning.

Reflection

Gratitude List

Our paths intertwine,
Like math, they align.
Two souls, time and again,
Find each other, like an old friend. Magnetic
pull so true,
With fate on our side,
let's let our love anew.

Reflection

Challenges are opportunities for growth and learning.

Reflection

Gratitude List

Love, a fulcrum's grace,
Perfect lever finds its place,
Balanced at love's base.

Reflection

I am exactly where I need to be.

Reflection

Gratitude List

Morning birds' sweet song,
Sun rays stretch shadows so long.
In sleep, toward the light, I sway,
Reaching to hold you,
but you're far away.
Dreams weave a world where you're near,
Waking brings the truth,

you said goodbye to me in September.

Reflection

I am exactly where I need to be.

Reflection

Gratitude List

Fall

on hearbreak

Reflection

I am worthy of love and respect.

Reflection

Gratitude List

Autumn leaves gently fall,
One by one, nature's silent call.
Each leaf tells a story of grief, Enduring, just to
stay in relief.

Bare branches in the quiet air,
No breeze, no movement to share. The world
turns barren, like my heart, Echoes of your
words, a painful part.

In the cold, I stand alone,
Heart panic, uncertainty sown.
Chill in the air freezes time,
A stillness, a moment so sublime.

Reflection

Today, I will let go of what I can't control.

Reflection

Gratitude List

The platinum ring that
wraps around my finger,
Is just as fragile as your ego.

Reflection

My mind is filled with positive and loving thoughts.

Reflection

Gratitude List

I didn't want to leave.
Trouble brewed like a strong wind,
bringing me to my knees.

We held on to love,
even with our troubled past.

I wish our love was meant to last.

Reflection

Every challenge I face is an opportunity to grow and improve.

Reflection

Gratitude List

There are layers upon layers of tissue paper lies,
and no matter how hard I try, the truth will not rise.

I retell your stories,
wondering if they were made-up tales I told myself before bed.

I look through old photographs as they become epitaphs of a life
that was.
A life dismissed.
I can no longer want your love for me to exist.

Gaping holes are more straightforward to heal
than the thousand little cuts, I feel.

Your feelings toward me change with the weather.
We are not birds of a feather,
we are too different to be.

Your words are the wind that causes oceans to spin.
When you spew your lies,
the soul leaves your eyes.

For years, you were never who you said you would be.
The pleas fell on deaf ears; we are not birds of a feather.
You are dead to me.

You cracked the foundation on which I stand.
The sedation from this life keeps me from clawing my eyes.

You are not a man.
The tissue paper lies
caused days' worth of cries.
Don't you worry about me.
My tears will dry.

Reflection

My life is a gift and I will make the most of it.

Reflection

Gratitude List

Down the rabbit hole,
Secrets tighten their hold.
Choking, a slow descent, Into darkness,
where we're sent.
Further down we fall,
Strangled, until we sprawl.
Crumbled on the ground,
Silent echoes, no sound.

Reflection

Today, I choose joy and happiness.

Reflection

Gratitude List

A second chance to explore our flame,
Watch as the sparks dance,
away from the blame.
The sparks turned to fire,
No longer safe and warm.
We danced too close,
and now we are burned.

Reflection

I believe in my abilities and potential.

Reflection

Gratitude List

A circle,
continuous and never-ending.
We exchanged vows,
the words never-bending.
A promise of forever,
on that fateful day in November,
I learned that your eyes,
were looking at____
The truth was never present,
now we are filled with resentment.

Reflection

My past does not define my future.

Reflection

Gratitude List

You treated me like a toy,
You ultimate Fuckboy.

Reflection

I radiate confidence, self-respect, and inner harmony.

Reflection

Gratitude List

We exposed our souls,
to become strangers again.

Reflection

Today, I will take steps toward my goals.

Reflection

Gratitude List

Whispers of vows, now fading, lament,
Storms silent rage within, torment,
Divorce blooms, necessity sent,
Hearts mend, though love once fervent,
In the quiet aftermath, growth is meant.

Reflection

I am in control of my actions and reactions.

Reflection

Gratitude List

A few degrees of change in the environment can make a beautiful snowfall,

an icy bitch.

Reflection

I release all doubts and embrace my potential.

Reflection

Gratitude List

Winter

On healing

Reflection

I am attracting abundance into my life.

Reflection

Gratitude List

In the quiet corners of grief,
where tears fall like rain,
A symphony of pain plays,
a melody of heartache and strain.
Divorce, a shattered mirror reflecting
broken dreams,
Yet within the fragments, a mosaic of
strength gleams.

Reflection

My life is full of purpose and meaning.

Reflection

Gratitude List

In my younger years, I would run from my fears.
Moving from state to city,
Never staying long enough for the pity.

I moved from home to an address to avoid the issues I did not want to address.

It was easier to pretend I was not the same girl who made the mistakes of her past.
I would rather wear a disguise and hope that the façade would last.

Time has moved on, and I've run out of costumes to try on.
I'm no longer young enough to run-
the hiding from my past has to be done.

Peeling back the layers I carried to hold myself back.

I'm no longer afraid of what will be
It's nice to be authentically me.

Reflection

I am surrounded by positive energy and I attract positive people.

Reflection

Gratitude List

Why did I ever flee,
From the person I was meant to be?

Reflection

I am enough just as I am.

Reflection

Gratitude List

Imagine if all the horses,
turned to the fences and came to their
senses.
In one moment they realized their own
strength,
and began to run at full length.
With all their smarts, they leaped over the
fences that held them back,
to freedom,
to a new start.

Reflection

Every day is a new opportunity for growth and progress.

Reflection

Gratitude List

Growing up too fast,
a carousel spinning wild,
Yet in the haste,
emerges a resilient child.

Learning life's lessons in the blink of an eye,

Creativity becomes a refuge,
a star in the sky.

Reflection

I am grateful for the gift of today.

Reflection

Gratitude List

There is no timing that is right,
even when we try with all our might.
All we can do is follow our heart,
Trusting that our life,
is God's art.

Reflection

I am at peace with all that has happened, is happening, and will happen.

Reflection

Gratitude List

God determines our path,
laying out our map at conception.
A math that only he knows,
our lives are not a prediction.
they are carefully curated and planned,
our souls are older than man,
intertwined with the collective whole,
when a human feels lost,
we must trust and learn to let go.

Reflection

I trust myself to make the right decisions.

Reflection

Gratitude List

On a branch, a bird, beauty in repose.
Others soared while she chose to close.
Her wings worked, yet she hesitated,
Nest's safety is a choice unabated.
A storm arrived, winds untamed,
Branches creaked, safety now maimed.
No sanctuary in that once-secure place,
In one swift gust, a destiny to face.
Branch split, and a forceful decree,
Forced her wings and claws set free.
Far she flew, danger behind,
Each flap shedding fears that bind.
In the vast expanse, her spirit untethers,
No longer afraid of the unknown.
Free, she soared, a dance with the sky,
The beautiful bird, no longer shy.

My potential to succeed is limitless.

Reflection

Gratitude List

I'm tired of my life being magnified.
My feelings being crucified.
My body being objectified.
It is time I rectify my life.
I will defy,
I will edify,
I will fly.

Reflection

I am a beacon of love and compassion.

Reflection

Gratitude List

Wounds whisper, now mend,
Gentle waves of time restore,
Healing's silent shore.

Reflection

I attract success and prosperity with each step I take.

Reflection

Gratitude List

I look at the scars that grace my hand,
each one a memory,
a story of my brand.
Visible, tangible, easy to see-
I wonder about the scars,
only visible to me?
How will I explain them,
as time moves on?
How will I let someone new know?
All the pain I carry,
all the stories I do not share.
will anyone care?

Reflection

I let go of fear and embrace love.

Reflection

Gratitude List

In my darkest hour,
I worry you were the best I'll ever do.
Until I remember,
you loved me for you.

Reflection

I am deserving of success and happiness.

Reflection

Gratitude List

Once upon a time, my heart's door swung
wide open,
Welcoming all, without a notion to be broken.
There were no tests to pass,
no need to prove,
There was no gatekeeper,
just freedom to move.
Fear and worry strolled right in,
Claiming space with a mischievous grin.
But upon reflection, a change emerged:
It is time to retreat; self-love is deserved.

Lacking self-compassion, anxiety's plea,
I took the reins and set myself free.
With care, I raised the drawbridge high,
Outlined new boundaries against the sky.
Saying no to anger, refusing hate's game,
Establishing limits, not more of the same.
Love flourished within, radiant and true,
No longer suffocating,
now embracing the view.

Reflection

My life is a canvas, and I am the artist.

Reflection

Gratitude List

Spring
on growth

Reflection

I am grateful for the abundance in my life.

Reflection

Gratitude List

Nature does not allow for broken things.
trees shed dead limbs,
to blossom in the spring.
Seasons shift for the earth to renew-
You will not break in hardship-
You simply will shed something old,
to expose you to something new.

Reflection

I have the power to create change.

Reflection

Gratitude List

When I was a young girl,
I learned to garden with my grandfather.
He taught me to sow the soil carefully,
Plant seeds of wisdom,
and water in the proper share.

A summer's journey,
the garden's gentle growth,
From emptiness to life,
a transformation to show.
Dirt in my hands, a memory so dear,
Roots planted in lessons, crystal clear.

As an adult, tending a garden anew,
The soil of life, a canvas to strew.
Seeds of creativity, ideas to sow,
My body is the garden,
where dreams can grow.
I water myself with inspiration's flow,
Creativity ablaze, ideas aglow.
Blossoming into the person meant to be,
In the garden of self, my spirit is free.

My grandfather's lessons are a guiding light,
In the bloom of adulthood, they take flight.
He sees, from wherever he might be,
The garden within me, a legacy.

Reflection

I am becoming a better version of myself every day.

Reflection

Gratitude List

You see those birds soaring high, living free,
But absolute freedom is found in trust,
can't you see?
Their instincts guide them through
migration's dance,
Braving winds together, it's a cosmic
romance.
With trust, they build a cozy and warm nest,
Facing storms together, weathering any
storm.
Wherever they fly, they make it their own,
In trust, they roam, never feeling alone.

Darling, it's your time to follow the wisdom
they bring,
Living freely and trusting is the real thing.
In trust, we find our freedom's sweet song,
It's a journey where we all belong.

Reflection

I am becoming a better version of myself every day.

Reflection

Gratitude List

Trees, reminders stand,
Lost branches, growth unfolds still,
Endless strength in roots.

My life is unfolding perfectly.

Reflection

Gratitude List

I planted a tiny vine in a large pot,
expecting it to shine.
Weeks passed, and no growth was in sight,
Leaves turned brown, losing their light.
I took the tiny vine,
Withered and brown, needing a sign.
In a smaller pot, hope applied,
Within a week, the vine revived.

I watched the vine as it thrived,
Realizing it was teaching me
a lesson about our lives.

If you are not growing,
Change your environment.

Reflection

I am worthy of respect and acceptance.

Reflection

Gratitude List

Dreams take flight, so high,
Logic grounds, stagnant below.
Balance keeps you afloat.

Reflection

I am a source of inspiration for others.

Reflection

Gratitude List

Anxiety's not the label we wear,
It just highlights the things we love, we care.
A spotlight on what needs a tweak,
When our hearts stray from the path we seek.
It's not an enemy in disguise,
But a gentle nudge to open our eyes
Not pushing what's false, just to construe,
Anxiety is a whisper, guiding me and you.

Reflection

I am a magnet for miracles, and I am open to receiving them.

Reflection

Gratitude List

As dawn breaks its gentle vow,
Sunrise whispers, "Here and now."
I rise up, dust off the pain,
Tomorrow's chance, I'll try again.

Reflection

I am resilient, and I can overcome any obstacle.

Reflection

Gratitude List

Our soul is a puzzle,
pieces varied from the soul's birth
guided by the heart,
each fragment finds it worth.

Passions unfold,
Dreams and heartbreaks untold.
Recovery's embrace,
Moments shaped by discovery's grace.

Reflection

I believe in the power of my dreams.

Reflection

Gratitude List

In the dance of ink, I find my flight,
Freedom's echo in the dead of night.
Like birds that soar on winds untamed,
Through writing's realm,
my soul's unchained.

Reflection

I am in the process of becoming the best version of myself.

Reflection

Gratitude List

Confidence isn't bought,
Nor gifted, nor sought.
It springs from within,
A self-nurtured kin.
Guard it from the fray,
No one can take it away.

Reflection

I am open to receiving love and kindness from others.

Reflection

Gratitude List

Beyond the surface, beyond the dress,
My soul defines, it's my true address.
In every moment, I confess,
Finding wholeness, nothing less.

Reflection

My life is a reflection of the love and positivity I radiate.

Reflection

Gratitude List

Did you know:

Before a hunt, penguins intentionally ruffle their
feathers.
It makes them faster against the cold water,
It gives them strength against the tide.

Feel free to ruffle my feathers,
I can brave any weather.
It might make my journey longer,
But you're just making me stronger.

Reflection

I am grateful for the lessons my challenges have taught me.

Reflection

Gratitude List

Anger does not form when someone hurts me:
A boundary does.

Reflection

I am grateful for the lessons my challenges have taught me.

Reflection

Gratitude List

I ponder the Titanic,
a colossal relic in the ocean's abyss.
Once a majestic beauty,
doomed to a fatal kiss.
Thousands met the tide,
unaware it was their last ride.
Decades pass, decay sets in,
Yet the Titanic births a new kin.

Now an ecosystem's embrace,
Life thrives in its sunken space.
Nature's resilience on display,
In Titanic's ruins, a thriving array.
Fish weave through cracks with ease,
In rogue boots, once adorned, life finds release.
Nature whispers secrets profound,
Beauty grows from darkness.

Reflection

I am confident in my abilities and trust my intuition.

Reflection

Gratitude List

Gratitude Prompts

- HEARTFELT COMPLIMENT RECEIVED
- SUPPORT FROM LOVED ONES
- SURPRISE GIFT
- KIND GESTURE
- SHARED WISDOM
- MEMORABLE TRAVEL EXPERIENCE
- DELICIOUS MEAL
- INSPIRING TALK
- TOUCHING ART/MUSIC
- DEVELOPED SKILLS/HOBBIES
- POSITIVE FEEDBACK
- DEEP CONNECTION
- RANDOM ACT OF KINDNESS
- FINANCIAL ASSISTANCE
- GUIDING ADVICE
- RESONATING BOOK
- COMFORTING EMBRACE
- GROWTH OPPORTUNITIES
- CHILDHOOD MEMORY
- TEACHER'S ENCOURAGEMENT
- PROFOUND LIFE LESSONS

- BREATHTAKING VIEW
- LISTENING EAR
- HEALING LAUGHTER
- ACCOMPLISHED CHALLENGE
- THOUGHTFUL LETTER
- NATURAL WONDER
- EDUCATIONAL OPPORTUNITIES
- FRIENDSHIP SUPPORT
- FAVORITE SONG OR ALBUM
- PERSONAL ACHIEVEMENTS
- FAMILY LOVE AND CARE
- INSPIRATIONAL ROLE MODEL
- PEACEFUL MOMENTS OF SOLITUDE
- MEMORABLE FAMILY GATHERING
- HELPFUL TECHNOLOGY OR TOOLS
- ACTS OF FORGIVENESS AND
  UNDERSTANDING
- JOYFUL MOMENTS OF LAUGHTER
- SUPPORTIVE AND LOVING COMMUNITY
- THE GIFT OF LIFE ITSELF

30 Days of Journal Prompts

Day 1: Describe your perfect day from start to finish.

Day 2: Write about a challenge you've overcome and how it has shaped you.

Day 3: List five things you're grateful for today and explain why.

Day 4: Reflect on a recent mistake or failure and what you've learned from it.

Day 5: Write a letter detailing your hopes and dreams for your future self.

Day 6: Describe a place that makes you feel calm and at peace.

Day 7: What are your top three priorities in life right now, and why?

Day 8: Write about a book or movie that has impacted you and why.

Day 9: What does self-care mean to you? How do you practice it?

Day 10: Reflect on when you felt proud of yourself and why.

Day 11: List three things you would like to accomplish next year and how you plan to achieve them.

Day 12: Write about a difficult decision you've had to make and how it has influenced your life.

Day 13: Describe your favorite childhood memory and why it's special to you.

Day 14: What are your biggest fears, and how do they affect your daily life

Day 15: Write a letter to someone who has made a positive impact on your life and thank them.

30 Days of Journal Prompts

Day 16: Reflect on a time when you felt overwhelmed. How did you cope with it?

Day 17: Describe your ideal future and what steps you can take to work towards it.

Day 18: Write about a hobby or interest that brings you joy and why.

Day 19: What would you like to improve about yourself, and how do you plan to do so?

Day 20: Write about a time when you felt inspired and motivated. What sparked this feeling?

Day 21: Reflect on a lesson you've learned recently and how it has changed your perspective.

Day 22: Describe someone who inspires you and why they are essential to you.

Day 23: Write about a time when you felt deeply connected to nature and the world around you.

Day 24: What are your favorite ways to relax and unwind after a long day?

Day 25: Reflect on a relationship important to you and why.

Day 26: Write about a goal you've achieved and how it has impacted your life.

Day 27: What things would you like to let go of or release from your life?

Day 28: Describe a moment when you felt delighted and content. Day 29: Write a list of affirmations or positive statements to boost your confidence and self-esteem.

Day 30: Reflect on the past month and write about any insights or lessons you've gained.

* 9 7 8 0 9 9 7 1 6 8 1 5 0 *